Black Mascara (Waterproof)
Rosalind Easton

smith|doorstop

the poetry business

Published 2021 by
Smith|Doorstop Books
The Poetry Business
Campo House,
54 Campo Lane,
Sheffield S1 2EG

Copyright © Rosalind Easton
All Rights Reserved

ISBN 978-1-912196-41-8
Typeset by The Poetry Business
Printed by People for Print

Smith|Doorstop Books are a member of Inpress:
www.inpressbooks.co.uk

Distributed by NBN International, 1 Deltic Avenue,
Rooksley, Milton Keynes MK13 8LD

The Poetry Business gratefully acknowledges the support of
Arts Council England.

Contents

7	Found in Translation
10	Campagnolo Super Record
12	Did I Dent Your Car with My Head?
13	Girl as Bike
14	Bra Fitting, Mayfair
15	Lunchtime on Threadneedle Street
17	The Light Museum
18	Drinks Party, London Skyline
19	The Music Stand
20	The Microphone
21	The Undiminished Magnificence of Brett Anderson
23	Tilda Swinton as David Bowie
24	Richard Burton and Elizabeth Taylor Take Over the Academy
26	Backstage
28	Closet
29	Peacock Suede Stilettos
30	Black Mascara (Waterproof)

for my nieces
Anabel, Georgia and Margot

Found in Translation

i.m. Nora Newton (1929–2015)

*A grandam's name is little less in love
than is the doting title of a mother;
they are as children but one step below ...*
                    Richard III

Of course I should have realised you'd come back
    as a book. It was in Hatchards on Piccadilly, in the Classics

section; the shelves were out of alphabetical order –
    Galsworthy, Trollope, Austen, Eliot side-by-side.

Just as I was thinking *I wonder*, I heard
    your laugh, and there you were – a slender, sparkling volume,

looking quite at home in such illustrious company,
    your handwritten name running down the spine. Evelyn Waugh

was serving at the till. *There's no charge*, he said.
    She's been waiting for you. I took you home and put you

next to Dickens and Gaskell, hoping you'd find some people there
    you could get on with. In the evenings I'd sit cross-legged on the carpet

with a glass of wine, listening, enthralled, to you in your element:
    on the poetry shelf, Milton's pages ruffled with pride to hear

that you'd learnt *Lycidas* by heart at seventeen; Wordsworth acknowledged
    that your annotations on 'The Prelude' had deepened his understanding.

Best of all was the intellectually superior drinking game
    with Shakespeare: he'd call out the number of a sonnet,

you'd recite it, word-perfect, your reward a shot of apricot brandy.
    You read my childhood favourites to me again, your drama-school voice

(not a trace of Manchester left in it) still just right, somehow, for
    The Famous Five and *Malory Towers*, but I liked your New Jersey drawl

for Judy Blume's *Freckle Juice* best, which brought you to the attention
    of George Gershwin and Judy Garland and Frank Sinatra

sleeping off champagne hangovers in Biography; the four of you sang
    'Embraceable You' and 'Someone to Watch Over Me' late into the night.

How sad, I thought, *that only in death can one keep this kind of company*.
    And then it struck me: I moved you to Plays. And oh, you were *away*.

Word spread quickly, and critics queued at my door, squeezed
    into every square inch in my small study, climbed lampposts

and garden fences to listen through the open window
    to your Lady Bracknell, your Rosalind, your Beatrice –

but also, of course, to your lead role in *Coronation Street*, and even
    the brief stint as first woman pundit on *Match of the Day*

(you always had the range). I realised then I'd put you in my library
    without reading your words, thought I knew your story, that I might

have written bits of it myself. But when I turned your pages
    there was your life translated: how you'd skipped rep altogether,

were plucked straight from training into your debut at the Old Vic;
    I saw the RSC, the National, the moody black-and-white photographs

backstage with Olivier, the sofa with Terry Wogan and Parkinson,
    the BAFTA red carpet, the BBC Four retrospective,

you refusing a ghostwriter and writing the bestselling memoirs yourself,
    Maggie Smith and Judi Dench taking calls from their agents –

Sorry, they've cast her again. I went back to Hatchards,
    and Evelyn Waugh. *How might we make this real?*

I asked. He lit his pipe, and smiled,
    and gestured at the sky. *No returns*, he said.

Campagnolo Super Record

Even when I asked for your number
it felt like swapping details at the scene
of an accident.

A year after you cleared the glass
from the road, paid off the bill,
filed away the witness statements,

I'm watching from the microclimate
of my Mercedes SLK as you dart
from a side road on your racer,

a fluorescent fish, too quick
for the protecting shoal
of the rush-hour peloton.

Here comes the double-decker,
a warship, cleaving the tarmac
into ripples, rolling you

out of the lane. Your face
registers the shock, the heart
beat in your throat, and you look

the way you looked the night
you found out I'd done
what I always knew I would do,

when your best friend and your sister
were paramedics, saying your name
as you shook the stars from your eyes

and tried to sit upright. But even after
the crunching pavement
of my final text, the crushed polystyrene

of ignoring your voicemails, I'm not sure
I can resist the jolt, the lurch, the slide
of recognition, that I won't

lean out, wave, call your name –

Did I Dent Your Car with My Head?

On the hottest day of the year, news breaks
of the first roundabout to give priority to cyclists.

                    This is just the beginning. As the week goes on
                    politicians grip lecterns, lean into microphones
                    to laud *hard-working couples without children.*

Supermarket shelf-edge labels belt out special offers
in red and white: *Buy Two, Pay For Two! Hovis is half price
only for the widow who takes one slice out of the freezer at a time!*

                    Lauren from Sidcup becomes the most expensive
                    care worker in history when she transfers
                    from Northbourne Court to Smyth Lodge for £100 million.

It is announced that men are more likely to die in an accident because cars
are crash tested for the average female body.
All manufacturers immediately recall and redesign.

                    And I steam straight onto the roundabout without looking,
                    slam my featherweight Italian carbon frame
                    into the ribcage of his 4x4,
                    send him somersaulting over the steering wheel,
                    ignore the red light blinking a distress signal on the tarmac
                    the empty shoe hanging upside down from the pedal
                    and the blood blooming through the elbows of his hi-vis jacket,
                    pick up his mangled car with its wheels
                    in the *calzone* position, hold it out to him and say
                    Hey, it's fine. You can drive it. Please don't tell the police.

Girl as Bike

The stethoscope answered in fluent Italian:
not a heartbeat, but the humming cadence
of a Campagnolo crankset. My father understood,

painted white lines around my cot, wrapped
childhood injuries in handlebar tape.
The moon's Anglepoise picked out

my race geometry: one knee raised, fists
loosely clenched, hands small enough
to forge tiny bikes from stretched-out paperclips

and roll them round a fruit-bowl velodrome.
In my teens, x-rays confirmed bones
of hollow carbon, ball bearings in the joints,

sinews and ligaments of fine steel cable.
So when I had to try four wheels and an engine
I kept energy bars in the glovebox,

insisted on an open sunroof in heavy rain.
My instructor asked *Why are you leaning
into the bends?* I told him if I couldn't sling it

over my shoulder and jog up a flight
of stone steps in Milan or Barcelona,
it wasn't for me. I sold the car,

spent the cash on seven kilos of hollow carbon,
the fluent Italian of a Campagnolo crankset,
tattooed an oily chainprint inside my right calf.

Bra Fitting, Mayfair

I wonder if this might be Lingerie Oz:
Toto, I don't think we're in Marks & Spencer anymore.
Behind the cubicle's red velvet drapes
the fitter twangs the backstrap of my bra
like David Gilmour appraising the strings
of a charity shop guitar.
I think of Oberon and Titania's elves, who,
for fear, creep into acorn cups and hide them there –
the fitter checks the label, laughs, then straps me
into something she says is a *moulded balcony,*
but seems to be a blue silk dragonfly's breath
as engineered by Isambard Kingdom Brunel.
Then when I read the size, and shriek with joy,
she swings me round to face the mirror –

and Coleridge, how right you were. For these
did Kubla Khan *a stately pleasure-dome decree;*
the film critic who wrote of Lara Croft
in Tomb Raider *a dead heat in a Zeppelin race*
might well have typed those lines for me,
and if I have a child I can offend Nigel Farage
with what he calls *breastfeeding ostentatiously –*
this means sparkly nipple tassels, one assumes,
and a playlist of appropriate showtunes
('Defying Gravity' from *Wicked,* obviously,
or Dolly Parton's 'Islands in the Stream') –
but, for now, there's only one song I need:
'Man! I Feel Like a Woman' by Shania Twain.
Let's go girls, she says. Well, yes. Indeed.

Lunchtime on Threadneedle Street

I'm waiting at a pedestrian crossing
remembering something I read
about traffic in 1920s New York:
how nobody was quite sure

if green meant *go* and how
absurd I found this
until the moment there you are
on the other side of the road

with a coffee cup (black filter,
one and a half sugars) and my feet
get stuck on red.
The sun's tungsten filament

crackles and fizzes
swings from the sky's ceiling
shakes loose
fragments of plaster-and-lathe cloud.

Under the tracing-paper layer of tarmac
the London clay judders an inch to the left
makes my iPhone flicker with
the ghost of a Nokia brick

and as I look at you – suit, tie, briefcase –
your negative held to the light
reveals faded Levi's, band T-shirt,
Adidas Gazelles, indie-boy hair.

I want the rain to come down
make your arms slick with water
make you wrap them around me again
but then you glance up, catch my look

and though your coffee ripples beneath its lid
it settles back again
and I see the woman with you
almost as young as we were

getting under your skin
in a way I can't, and never could.

The Light Museum

after Suzannah Evans

Please be advised that you look directly at our exhibits
at your own risk. Those with hangovers should wear
a blindfold and download the audio guide.

We begin with *Glare*, an exhibition specially curated
for those seeking an immersive light experience:
the torchlight from the Watergate scandal, on loan

from the LM in Washington DC;
a 150bpm pulse of unrepentant neon, believed
to originate from a pair of rave-era glowsticks.

In our endangered section, a square of starlight
cut from the London sky, presented here
expertly restored to its pre-industrial glory.

Next, our *Hollywood Circles* room: the pearl sheen
in which Judy Garland took her bow; the glow
from Ava Gardner's last cigarette, preserved intact.

Our interactive *Nostalgia* display lets you dive into
the colour of an early Beach Boys song, or watch again
the best sunset from your USA holiday in 1998,

scooped up from the bottom of the Grand Canyon.
(Small vials can be purchased from the gift shop,
priced at one year of your left life.)

Drinks Party, London Skyline

St Paul's arrives first, settles into
the quiet dignity of a small sherry,

looks on as the younger towers pile in all at once, slinging back
the Jägerbombs, demanding space and comparing reflections.

(St Paul's is unfazed by this, having spent
much of the 1940s flicking incendiary bombs
off its shoulders like specks of dandruff.)

The cranes dangle canapés and trays of drinks, stoop
to collect the empties.

Only they notice when the Gherkin, ashamed
of its 360-degree beer belly, tucks itself behind
22 Bishopsgate, sticks to lime and soda all night.

The Shard, the Scalpel and the Cheese Grater form a punk band,
slash holes in the sky and fasten them with safety pins,

while the Walkie Talkie and the Boomerang pass wraps
of powdered moonlight back and forth across the river.

The next morning, still drunk, still high, they all swap places to confuse
the passing commuters. How they giggle, delighted with their wheeze.

Only St Paul's, sipping strong black coffee
and smoking a Player's Navy Cut, is sober enough
to know nobody will be able to tell.

The Music Stand

Hear the creak of the garage door opening,
its dialogue with your aching joints,
rusted into this position by her doctor's insistence
that she must not sing pending the slow unbending,
unfolding movement of her referral letter up the long
ENT waiting list. Notice the weight lost from your frame
after months of neglect, once built with a certain
spindly, angular grace, the cracked mirror now
reflecting dismemberment, remembering
how she flung your lower section in grief and anger
behind the broken fridge. Lift your arm
to shield your face from the sun;
wait for the clear chime of contact between
the pieces of your broken body as she gathers
ribs and spine, carries you from the scene of the crash
into the house. Listen to her sigh in the study,
her small hands loosening and limbering
your slim limbs, spreading the music's sweeping
wings against the strong, broad bones of your back.
Track the skylark from the garden through the open window
till it perches on your shoulder. Feel the feather of her
barely-captured first breath as it settles on your palm.

The Microphone

Remember how you used to stand
alone together in her small room.
Understand it's bound to be awkward
after so long, relearning this pas de deux
from the beginning; keep your
back straight even as she gets the steps
wrong at first, adjusts her own height
instead of yours. Picture grainy
black and white, the ghosts of voices
past leaning in, the 1940s New York
nightclub smoke. Hold your breath
as she places an unrehearsed hand
on the nape of your neck; give in
to the moment she tilts your head
and now, at last, meets your gaze
and holds it. Hope you'll know
what to do when she lets both hands
drop to your waist and pulls you
to her, allows the left to glide
up your spine and then rest, where
it often did, on your face. Listen
as she falls easily into the secret
language you spoke together,
known only to the two of you,
heard only by the headphones.

The Undiminished Magnificence of Brett Anderson

Shepherd's Bush Empire, 20th November 2019

Side A

Press play. The solid click and analogue hiss is the sound
of teenage years that can't be overwritten with tiny pieces
of tape to cover the holes, not when he's flicking his hair,
still slick, still dark, still there, making the front row wet
with glorious Brett sweat, not when the low-slung thunder
of Richard's Gibson Les Paul Custom lets the 'Animal Nitrate' riff
out of its cage and we thrill to the rumble as it prowls
the stage, not when Brett unwinds the long lead

Side B

of the mic and whirls it above his head, pulling tight
the tangled length of memories we'd chucked in our bags
so they snagged on other things, making them spin
on the reels again, taking us back to writing his name
in Tipp-Ex on our cherry 1460s, being late for school
to go to Our Price on the morning of release, when all our days
to come were stacked to the ceiling like blank TDKs,
when we didn't know it's all felt-tipped in black, won't fade,
grow slack, and if you don't press stop

sometimes there's a hidden track

Tilda Swinton as David Bowie

Vogue Italia, February 2003

This was the line-up on the rail at the photographer's studio:
Ziggy Stardust, Aladdin Sane, the Thin White Duke,
Orlando as a boy, Orlando as a girl, Vita, Virginia.
At the shutter's click, you met under a streetlight
on the Reeperbahn, stayed up all night, fell asleep
at dawn in each other's arms and woke on a bed
of oak leaves in the garden at Knole,
played guitar and sang as I was born with my hair
on fire. In Paris, we held hands in an artist's impression
of the street that will take my name after I am gone;
in Berlin, we danced in the watchtower's shadow,
passed like Gitanes smoke right through the Wall. Now,
in this London winter, I stand on Southwark Bridge
and still the waters with the *Life on Mars* blue
of my breath. Cast off your layers – spaceman,
suit and tie, doublet and hose, breeches and gaiters,
string of pearls, ink where blood should flow –
until you are invisible. Step out onto the ice,
carve your names with the blades of your skates,
overwrite one with another until you have made
a new language – and as you watch the freezing
and melting of these curves and lines and try
to decipher their meaning, ask yourselves, honestly:
am I not the most beautiful thing you have ever seen?

Richard Burton and Elizabeth Taylor Take Over the Academy

A long-lost extract from the Richard Burton Diaries, found under the floorboards at his house in Switzerland

Monday

Woke in foul temper. Private jet and limo to school. Had blazing row with E over which one of us would be Head, but in the end I relented and agreed to be Deputy. Drank sixteen Martinis between us and smashed computers to bits with cricket bats. Placed large order with Hatchards and told them to put it all on my account.

Tuesday

Advertised in *Times Ed. Supplement* for new PA and received over 45,000 applications. E has torn up all the exercise books, declared the ballpoint pen an abomination, and sent the Head Boy to Smythson of Bond Street with her credit card.

Wednesday

No-notice safeguarding inspection from Ofsted, prompted by E waking up late and taking assembly in what she happened to be wearing at the time, namely her *Suddenly Last Summer* white swimsuit and a silk peignoir I bought for her birthday. Fortunately she was able to buy the inspectors off with some of her more ordinary diamonds and tickets to the premiere of *Who's Afraid of Virginia Woolf.*

Thursday

Drank Bloody Marys all day and went for late night dip in school pool. Large assembly of mothers gathered in viewing gallery, many of them insensible with excitement. Held job interviews for new Drama teacher but none of them a better Lear or Hamlet than me, so threw them all out and resolved to take the classes myself.

Friday

After a week locked in the library with me, my books and no computers nearly all students are now fluent in French and Russian and able to recite most of Shakespeare from memory. Model for school now being copied, with great success, around the country. Education Secretary's impotent fury a source of great delight.

Backstage

After Julia Copus

Three hours and twenty-five years ago,
she looked into this mirror and saw her –
someone she's always been, but doesn't know.
She wipes away kohl and greasepaint, switches off
the lights around the edge. For the last time,
the ones who begged her to stay are
calling her name at the stage door, waiting for her
with memories of nights she wants to forget;
she knows this means there's nothing left but
a false eyelash choking in an ashtray,
a laddered stocking drowning in the sink.
Somehow, the cards and flowers make her feel like
a drink (just one, to take the edge off
listening to her old songs and now the voices
of ghosts who drift in and out of dressing rooms).
Her overdue admission to the chorus line
all those years ago seems barely real. This is
the rest of her life stretched out before her.

The rest of her life stretched out before her
all those years ago seems barely real; this is
her overdue admission to the chorus line
of ghosts who drift in and out of dressing rooms,
listening to her old songs. And now the voices:
a drink. Just one, to take the edge off.
Somehow, the cards and flowers make her feel like
a laddered stocking drowning in the sink,
a false eyelash choking in an ashtray;

she knows this means there's nothing left, but
with memories of nights she wants to forget
calling her name at the stage door, waiting for her,
the ones who begged her to stay are
the lights around the edge. For the last time,
she wipes away kohl and greasepaint, switches off
someone she's always been, but doesn't know.
She looked into this mirror and saw her
three hours and twenty-five years ago.

Closet

You imagined emerging in full drag king regalia, perhaps swishing a superhero cape embroidered with k.d. lang lyrics and intertwined Venus symbols, then smashing it to pieces with a rainbow-striped axe – but you'd only just shut the door and settled in after years in the pre-closet holding pen, where your waist-length hair, collection of Royal Ballet programmes and the tears you cried at Scott and Charlene's wedding were Exhibits A, B and C in the Court of Why You Cannot Possibly Belong Here, and the case for the defence rested solely on the remote control you held your thumb over when you watched the Beth and Margaret kiss in Brookside with the sound turned low and one eye on the door, as you had destroyed all evidence of the breath that caught in your throat when your best friend was shut in her room with her boyfriend and you realised it wasn't her you were jealous of – so it was years before someone broke the padlock and dragged you out to make you understand all this, at which point you wrote to everyone who had to know but already knew (you would like to thank Bombay Sapphire for their generous sponsorship of this event), only to find it still in the corner of the room the next morning, fitted with a revolving glass door for those moments when the plumber or your driving instructor asks what your husband does, and when it spins at top speed you see, again and again and again, the fifteen-year-old girl who's still in there, and can't come out.

Peacock Suede Stilettos

This is exactly how she unwrapped your heart. She found its hiding place, drew back the lid, unfolded the tissue paper with such tender curiosity she didn't realise she had a sharp blade up her sleeve. Remember now, as autumn looks over its shoulder, pulls its scarf tighter against winter's bitter breath, the summer's height. That night. The black skinny jeans and silver top, the shimmer and the snap of your Clinique compact. The left and then the right. The front door's click. The moment your heels hit the pavement burning with the August sun, and just how carefully you picked your way over this new ground, the cracks and stones that might have made you trip, the long grass turning yellow at the tips. How you thought this was the night she might have felt it too. But she'd go, leave, move away to be with her man the way they alw ays do.

Black Mascara (Waterproof)

I have a wand. This is misleading:
it casts no spell to conjure in her
feelings that she doesn't have.

You put me in your handbag
as though going into battle
with the love you tried to hide.

In your chest there was a reservoir
where the water's fingers
had been clinging on for months,

and you thought I was
your Hoover Dam, your sandbag wall
for holding back the tide

that surged inside you
even as you pressed a thumb
against the waterfall.

But in that place where oceans meet
powder and foundation slide away
and her utter gone-ness is complete.

Now I'm all that you have left
there's no point in me being waterproof.
You might as well have bought the kind

that leaves black rivers
running down your face:
at least they'd tell the truth.

Acknowledgements

I would like to thank Imtiaz Dharker and Ian McMillan for selecting me as one of the winners of the 2020 International Book & Pamphlet Competition, and for their wonderful comments.

Working with my editor, Peter Sansom, has been an enriching and enjoyable experience. I am new to the poetry world, and Peter's comments and insights were instrumental not only in bringing the collection together, but also in my development as a poet. Sincere thanks are due to him.

I would also like to thank the editors of *Fragmented Voices* and *The Alchemy Spoon*, in which two of these poems ('Campagnolo Super Record' and 'Lunchtime on Threadneedle Street' respectively) were first published.

Finally, huge thanks to everyone at The Poetry Business for making this happen.

Stanza five of 'Did I Dent Your Car with My Head?' reverses the genders of a statistic taken from *Invisible Women: Exposing Data Bias in a World Designed for Men* by Caroline Criado Perez (Chatto and Windus, 2019).

The first two stanzas of 'Lunchtime on Threadneedle Street' refer to Sarah Churchwell's book *Careless People: Murder, Mayhem and the Invention of The Great Gatsby* (Virago, 2013).

'Richard Burton and Elizabeth Taylor Take Over the Academy' includes phrases from *The Richard Burton Diaries* (ed. by Chris Williams, Yale University Press, 2013).